THE EUGÉNIE ROCHEROLLE SERIES

Intermediate Piano Solo

Rodgers & Hammerstein
Selected Favorites

8 Piano Solos Arranged by Eugénie Rocherolle

ISBN 978-1-4234-8764-7

Copyright © 2009 by WILLIAMSON MUSIC
International Copyright Secured   All Rights Reserved

Williamson Music is a registered trademark of Imagem, C.V.
Rodgers and Hammerstein and the R&H logo are trademarks of Imagem, C.V.

www.rnh.com

WILLIAMSON MUSIC®
A RODGERS AND HAMMERSTEIN COMPANY
www.williamsonmusic.com

EXCLUSIVELY DISTRIBUTED BY
HAL•LEONARD®
CORPORATION
7777 W. BLUEMOUND RD. P.O. BOX 13819 MILWAUKEE, WI 53213

Visit Hal Leonard Online at
www.halleonard.com

DO-RE-MI
from THE SOUND OF MUSIC

Music by RICHARD RODGERS
Lyrics by OSCAR HAMMERSTEIN II
Arranged by Eugénie Rocherolle

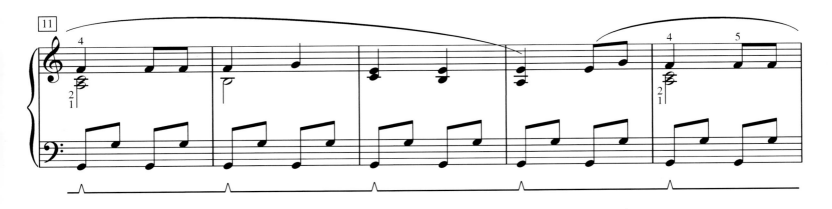

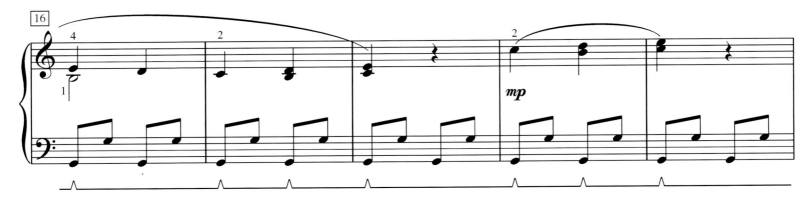

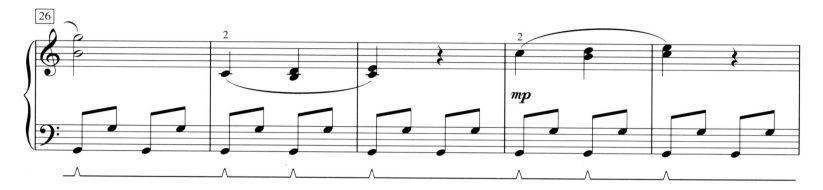

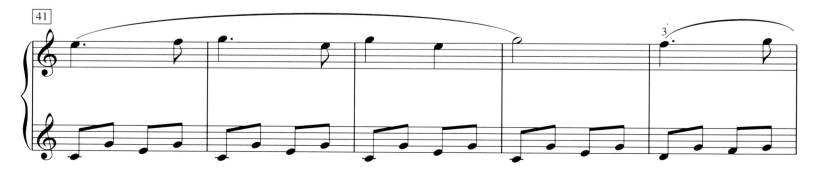

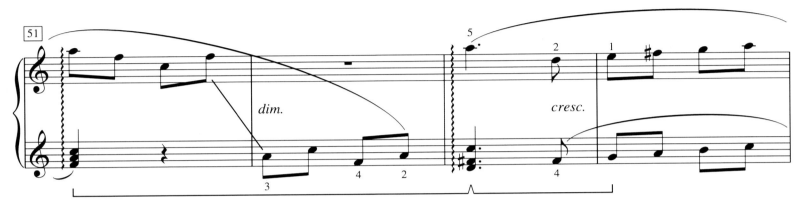

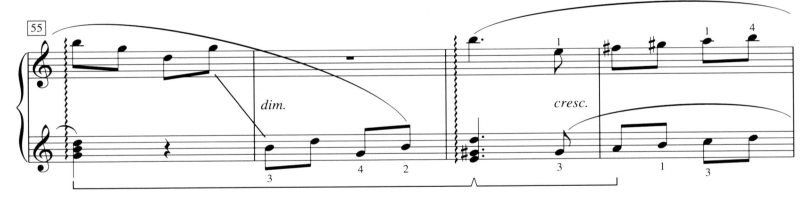

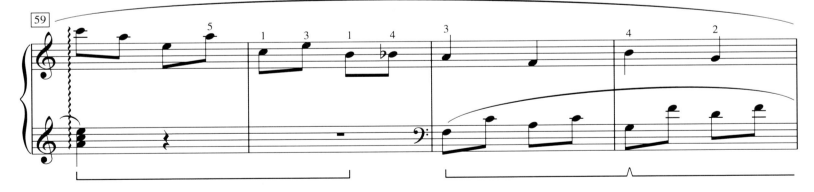

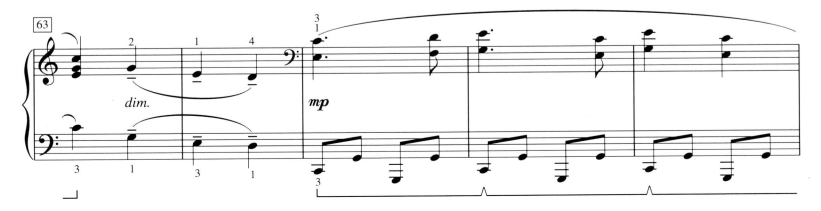

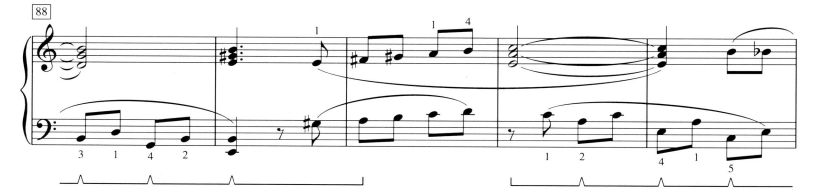

6

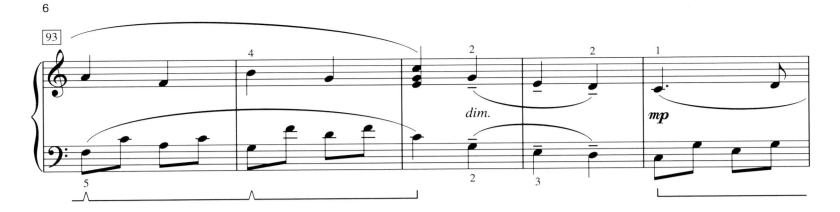

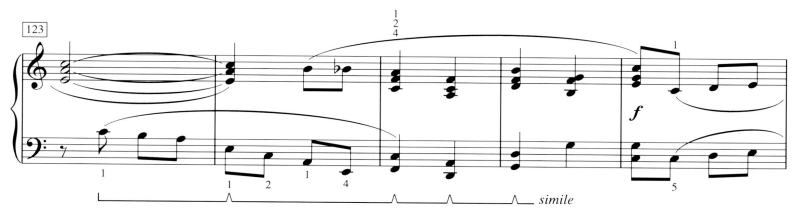

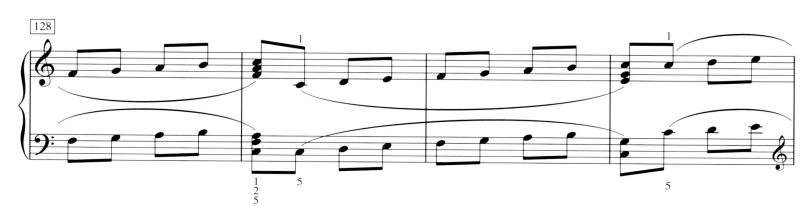

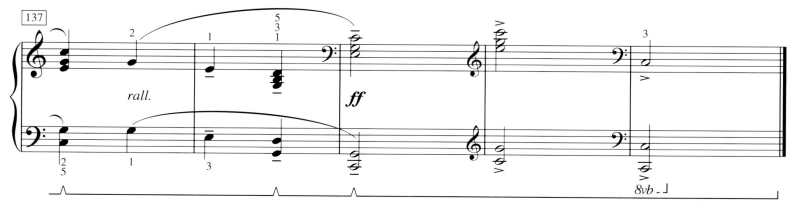

CLIMB EV'RY MOUNTAIN
from THE SOUND OF MUSIC

Music by RICHARD RODGERS
Lyrics by OSCAR HAMMERSTEIN II
Arranged by Eugénie Rocherolle

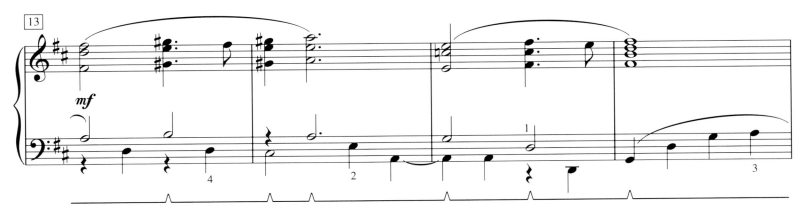

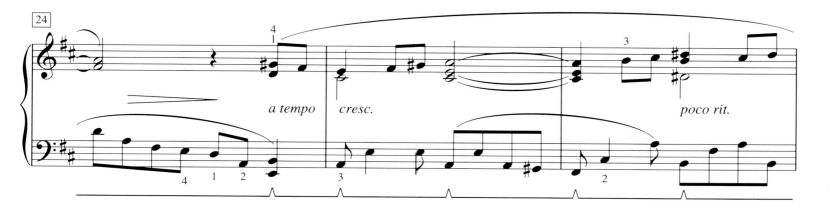

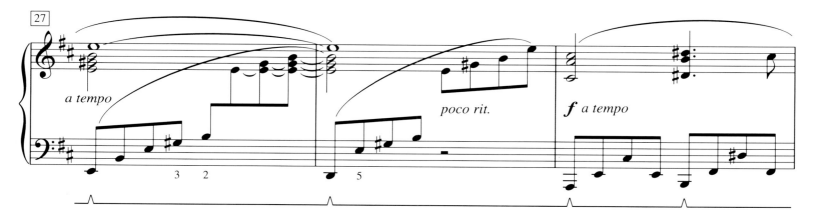

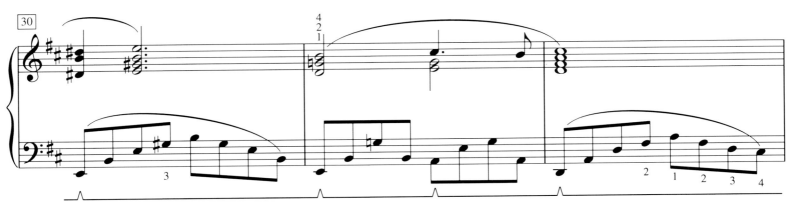

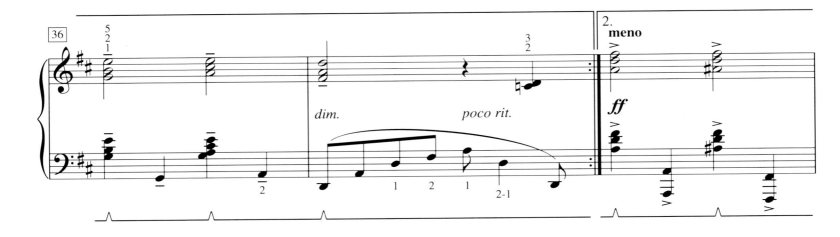

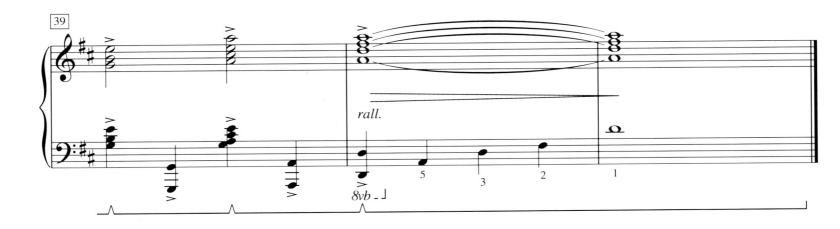

IF I LOVED YOU

from CAROUSEL

Lyrics by OSCAR HAMMERSTEIN II
Music by RICHARD RODGERS
Arranged by Eugénie Rocherolle

Moderato (♩ = 120)

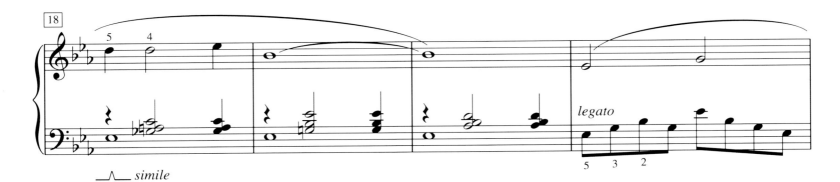

simile

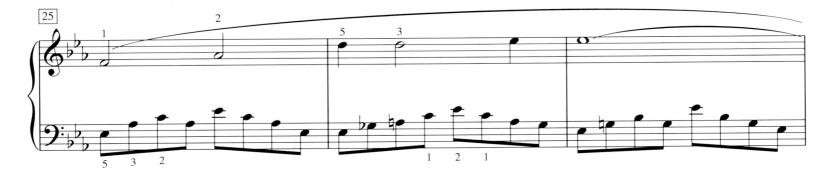

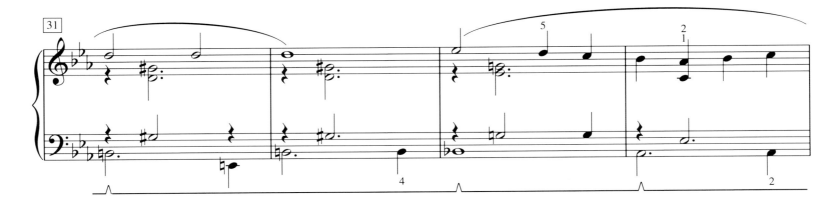

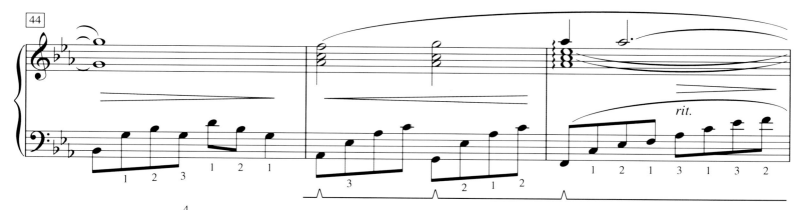

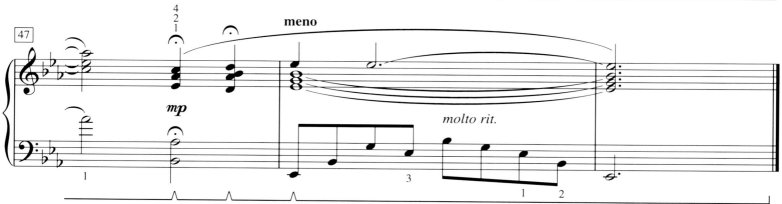

OKLAHOMA

from OKLAHOMA!

Lyrics by OSCAR HAMMERSTEIN II
Music by RICHARD RODGERS
Arranged by Eugénie Rocherolle

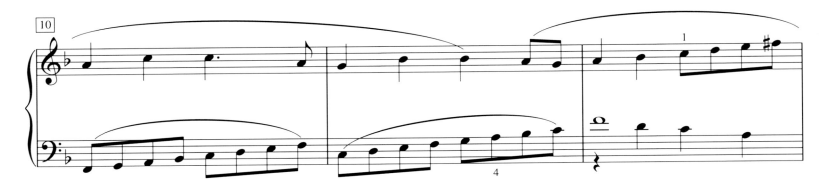

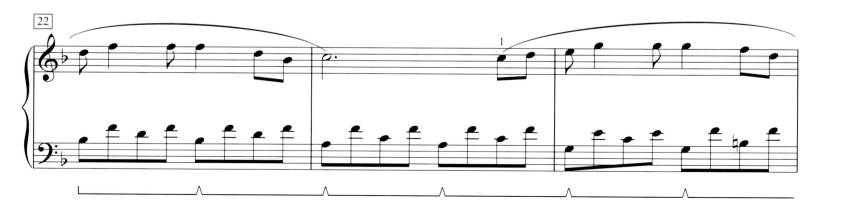

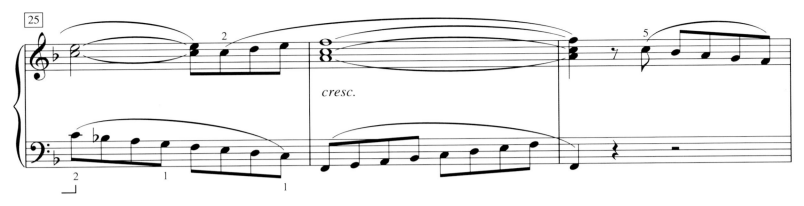

THERE IS NOTHIN' LIKE A DAME

from SOUTH PACIFIC

Music by RICHARD RODGERS
Lyrics by OSCAR HAMMERSTEIN II
Arranged by Eugénie Rocherolle

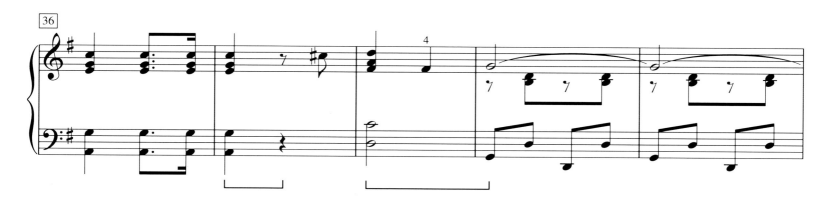

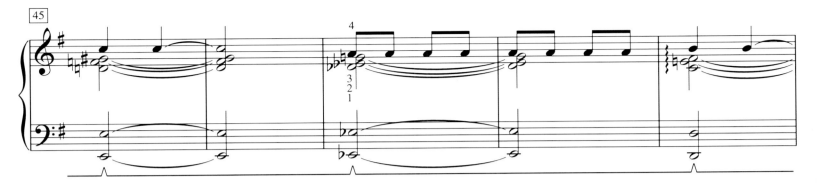

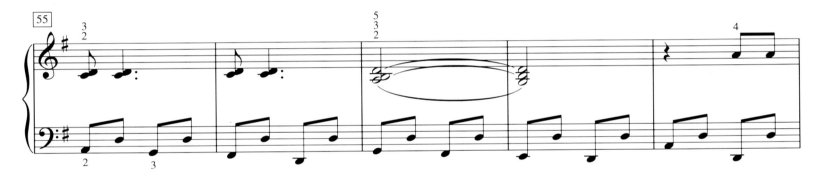

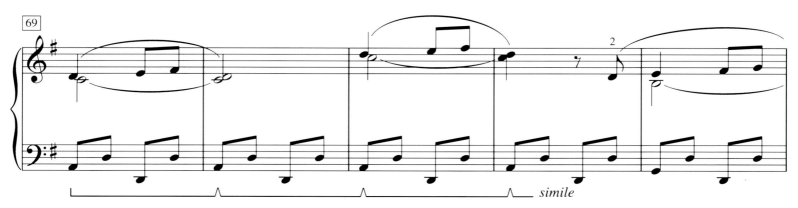

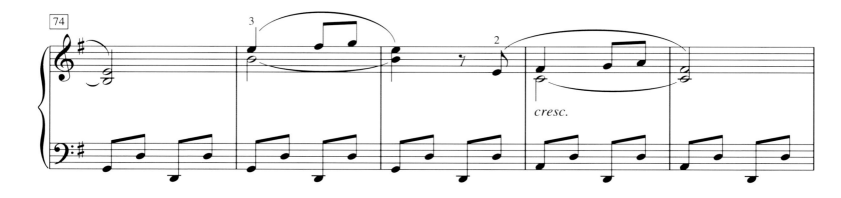

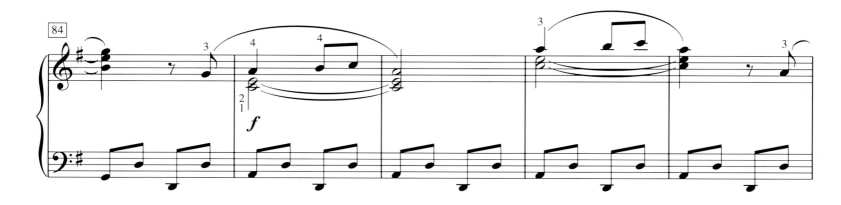

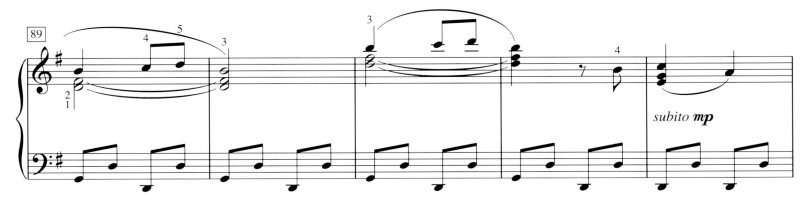

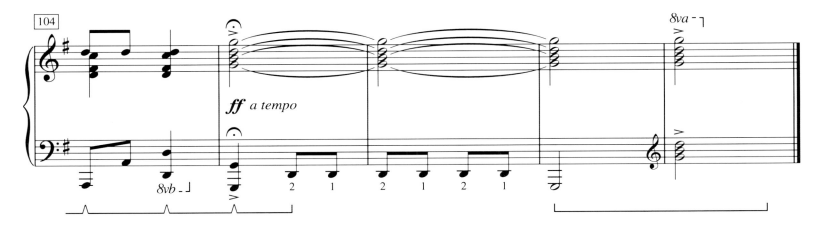

SHALL WE DANCE?

from THE KING AND I

Lyrics by OSCAR HAMMERSTEIN II
Music by RICHARD RODGERS
Arranged by Eugénie Rocherolle

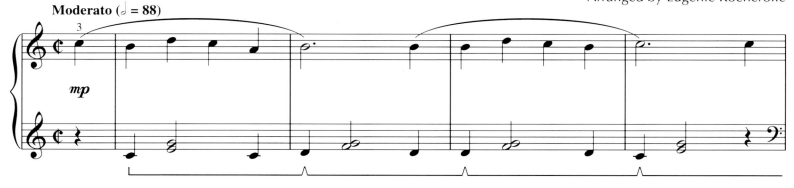

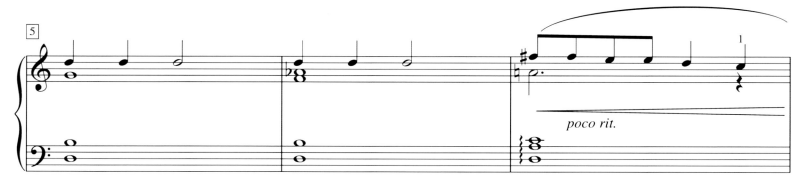

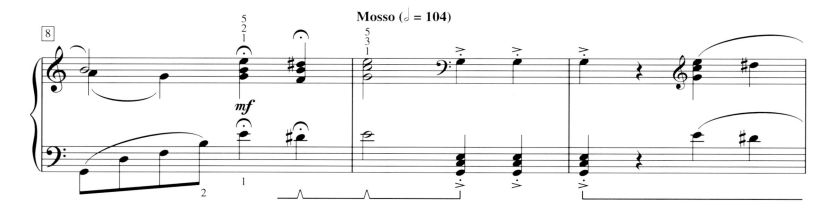

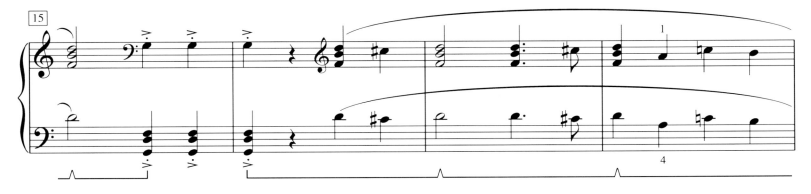

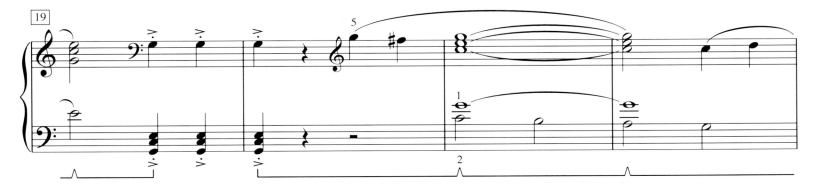

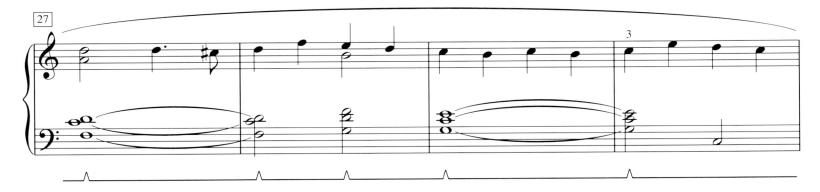

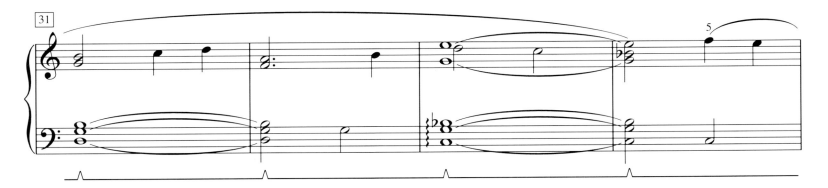

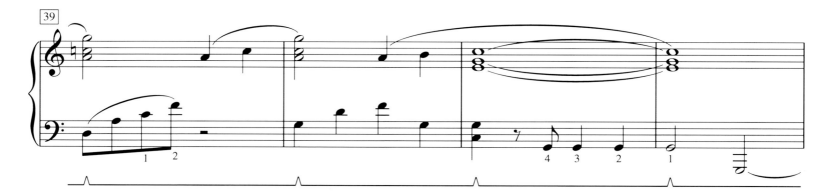

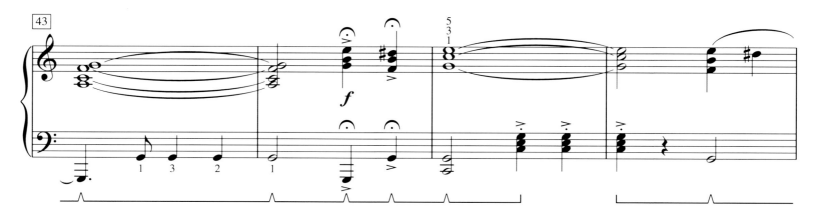

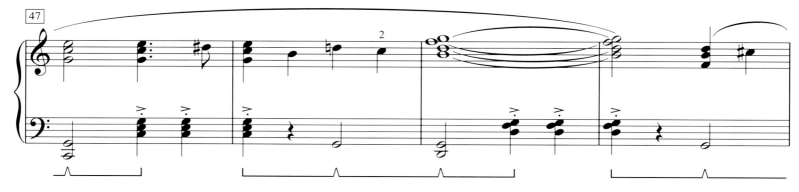

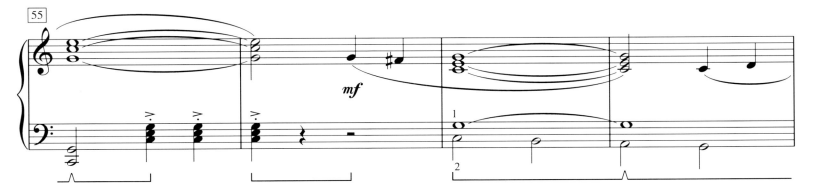

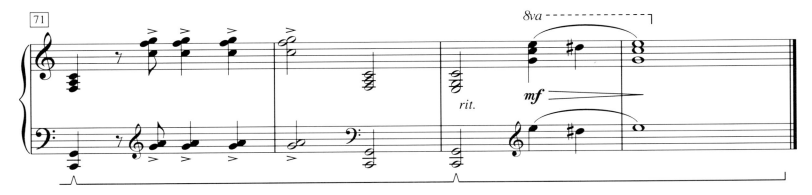

SOME ENCHANTED EVENING

from SOUTH PACIFIC

Lyrics by OSCAR HAMMERSTEIN II
Music by RICHARD RODGERS
Arranged by Eugénie Rocherolle

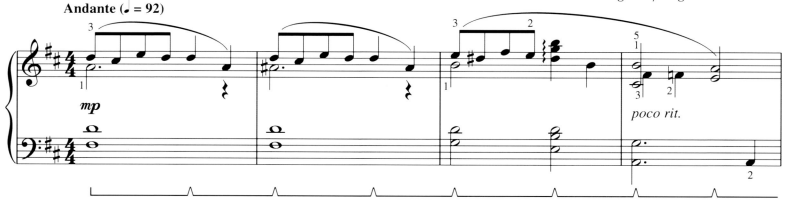

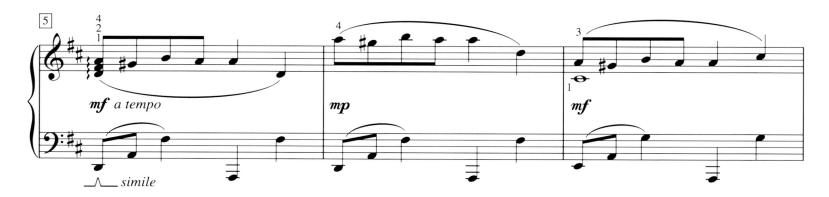

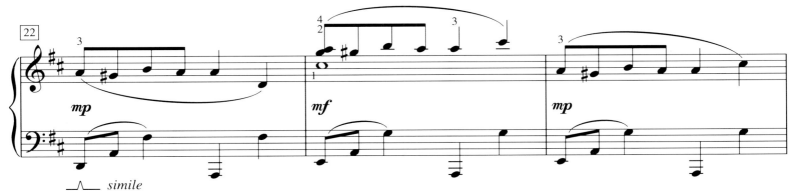

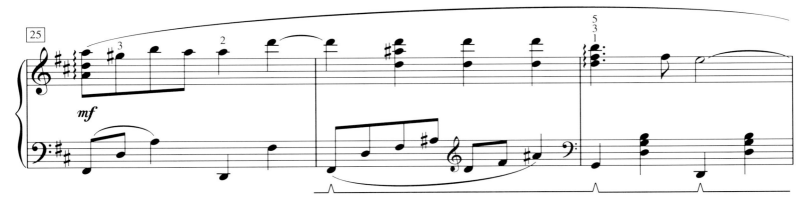

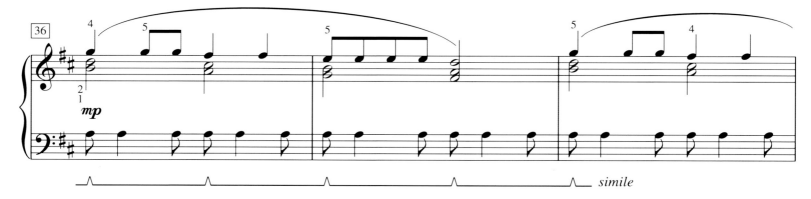

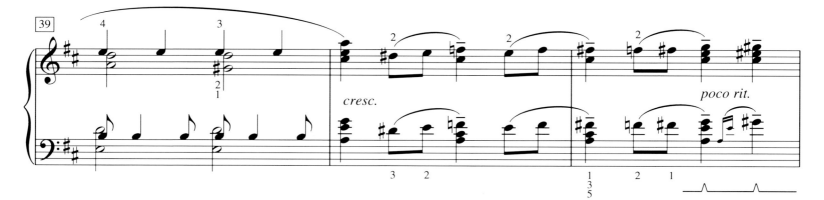

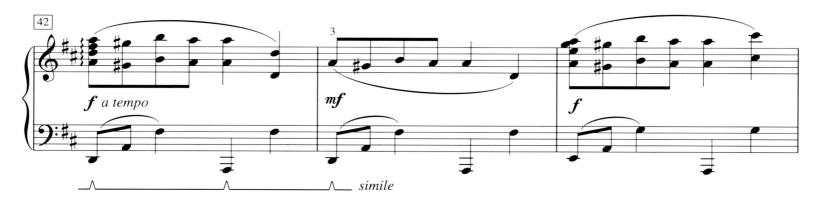

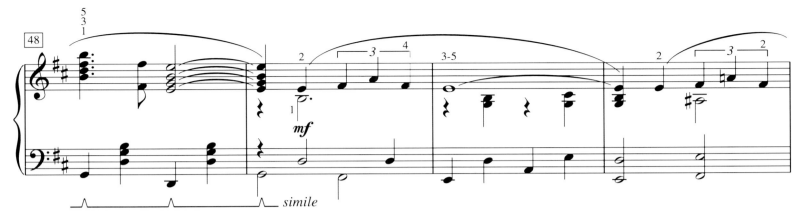

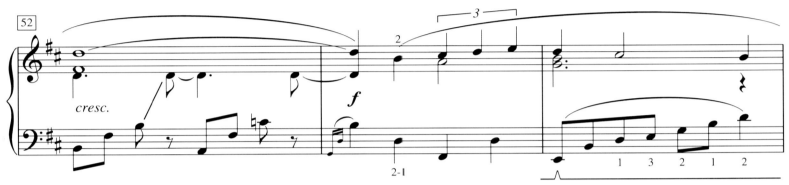

YOU'LL NEVER WALK ALONE

from CAROUSEL

Lyrics by OSCAR HAMMERSTEIN II
Music by RICHARD RODGERS
Arranged by Eugénie Rocherolle

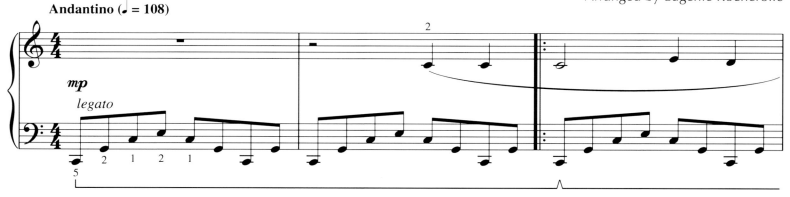

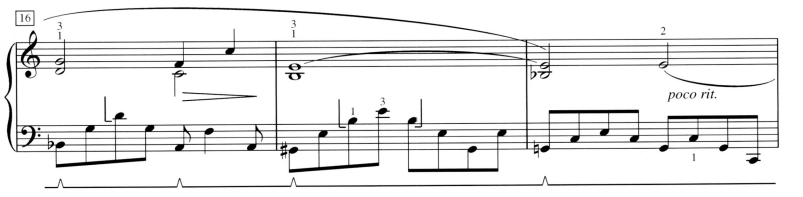

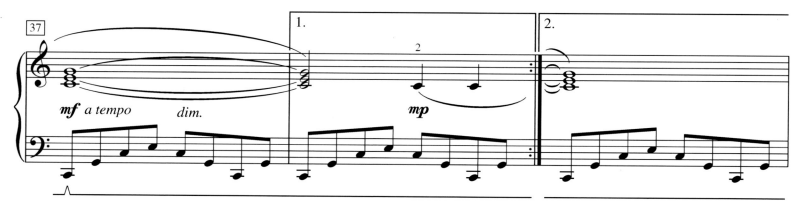